P9-CLE-549

HOLOCAUST BIOGRAPHIES

Adolf Hitler
A Study in Hate

Jeremy Roberts

THE ROSEN PUBLISHING GROUP, INC.
NEW YORK

943.086
ROB

Published in 2001 by The Rosen Publishing Group, Inc.
29 East 21st Street, New York, NY 10010

Copyright © 2001 by The Rosen Publishing Group, Inc.

First Edition

All rights reserved. No part of this book may be reproduced
in any form without permission in writing from the
publisher, except by a reviewer.

Library of Congress Cataloging-in-Publication Data

Roberts, Jeremy, 1956–
    Adolf Hitler: a study in hate/by Jeremy Roberts.—1st ed.
        p. cm.—(Holocaust biographies)
    Includes bibliographical references and index.
    ISBN 0-8239-3317-2 (lib. bdg.)
    1. Hitler, Adolf, 1889–1945. 2. Heads of state—Germany—
Biography. 3. Holocaust, Jewish (1939–1945) 4. National
socialism. 5. Germany—Politics and government—1933–1945.
I. Title. II. Series.
DD247.H5 A35828 2000
943.086'092—dc21

                                              00-010506

Manufactured in the United States of America

Contents

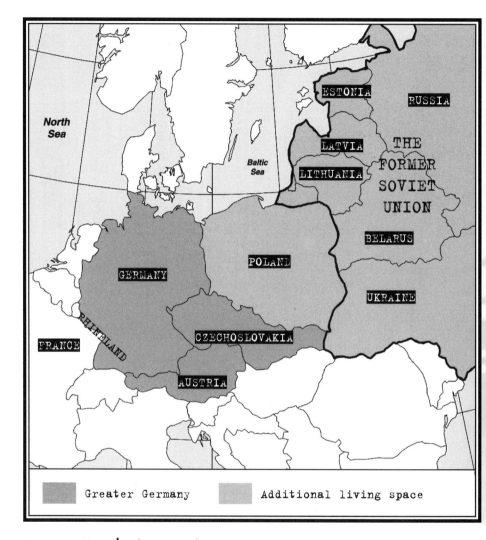

Map of Hitler's (original) conquest. A plan to restore the borders
of Greater Germany and to add living space in the East (in 1936)

Introduction: War and Hate

It was November 1918. The corporal sat in the hospital chair, dumbfounded, as the pastor spoke. The Great War was over. Germany's Kaiser had abdicated, giving up his claim to be leader. A new government was taking over. It would be a democracy.

To the corporal, it seemed the world had turned upside down. Germany had given up at the edge of victory. Four years of horrible war had been for nothing. He stumbled back to his bed, tears welling in his eyes. He had been temporarily blinded by British mustard gas a few days before. This felt a million times worse.

The soldier's name was Adolf Hitler. Millions of Germans shared his dismay. The anger and disappointment they felt would shape world history for decades to come.

A Flesh and Blood Devil

Many people were responsible for the Holocaust, in which millions of Jews and others were murdered. But no one person bears as much guilt as Adolf Hitler. Hitler was the absolute leader of Germany in the 1930s and 1940s. He made the persecution of Jews official government policy. His wishes led to millions and millions of deaths.

Hitler rose to power by preaching hate, violence, and murder. He won support by telling lies and encouraging prejudice. He waged war in the name of racial purity. To us, he seems an inhuman monster. He seems the devil himself. But Hitler was flesh and blood. His hate was terrible and his logic twisted. But it is all the more frightening because that hate is not so different from the emotions many other humans feel even today.

The Germany of Hitler's time was unique. It helped make Hitler and the Holocaust possible. But it was not so different that we don't recognize it as a human society.

Hitler and Germany began on their horrible path together at the end of a terrible war. In a little less than twenty years, Hitler would begin an even more terrifying war. And that war would lead to one of the worst crimes mankind has ever committed, the Holocaust.

1. A Stab in the Back

Adolf Hitler was born in a small Austrian town on April 20, 1889. He wanted to be an artist as a young man. After his father died, he moved to Vienna to pursue this dream. But he failed the entrance exam to the art school twice. At one point, he was so poor he had to beg at a homeless shelter. Finally he managed to make a living selling small paintings and postcards. He moved to Munich, Germany, in 1913 after receiving a small inheritance.

Like many Austrians who lived near the German border, Hitler's family had German roots. Like many, Hitler thought of himself as German, not Austrian. When war broke out in Europe in 1914, he joined the German army. He

Hitler (left) as a soldier during World War I

won two medals for bravery. He was promoted to corporal. On the other hand, Hitler did not seem destined for greatness in the army. No one thought of him as a great leader.

Disappointment

Germany did well when the war began. The country surprised France with a massive invasion in 1914. But by the summer of 1918, France and Britain began to win important victories. Behind the lines, Germany had been drained by years of war and a blockade that prevented it from receiving supplies. There was a severe lack of food and other necessary items.

The Kaiser and his government soon realized that surrender was the only way to prevent foreign troops from swarming through Germany. Giving up seemed the best way to prevent more suffering. More importantly, it would prevent a disastrous revolution. Russia had been defeated the year before after just such a revolution. The civil war that followed the revolution brought communists to power and caused even more suffering.

Many Germans, however, didn't realize how near defeat their country was. German armies were still on foreign soil. Momentum had shifted back and forth many times during the past four years. Some soldiers felt they were winning. Others felt that they could win, if they just kept fighting. The surrender struck them as a betrayal.

The new government that took over Germany negotiated a peace agreement. Hitler thought the men who formed the government were all criminals. He and others called the surrender a "stab in the back." Their anger remained with them long after the war ended.

A Home in the Army

Until he joined the army, Hitler's future seemed dim. In some respects, the army was the best home he had ever known. So Hitler stayed in the army even after the war. He won a transfer to Munich, where he had lived before.

Munich was part of the German state of Bavaria. Immediately after World War I, different factions vied for control. There were riots and uprisings. At the same time, there were many hardships. Food, coal, and other necessities were in short supply. Political turmoil soon led to a revolution headed by local communist groups. In April, these forces took over the Bavarian government. They formed a Red army. Chaos and anarchy reined. By May, these revolutionaries had been defeated with the help of the central government, the army, and volunteer *Freikorps* troops. One of these groups wore "fire whisks" on their helmets, symbols of the earth's creation. Today we know the symbol as a swastika; the Nazis would adopt it some years later.

At first, Hitler was not very involved in the politics or the chaos of Munich. His job as a soldier was mostly to test gas masks. But he soon became involved in politics, perhaps starting as a representative for his army unit. When the Red revolution was put down, Hitler quickly became known as an anticommunist and nationalist.

At the time, the army played an important role in politics. Officers organized against the communists. Hitler began taking classes and attending lectures on German nationalism, economics, and other matters. He lectured

A picture from an anti-Semitic German children's
book portrays a group of Jews as crooks.

other soldiers on the war and Germany's
future. Among his common themes was the
claim that Jews had caused Germany to lose
the war. He said they were responsible for the
"stab in the back."

Anti-Semitism

Jews had served in the army in great numbers.
As a group, Jews were no different than other

German citizens. Some were very patriotic, others not. Some were well-to-do, others poor. The idea that Jews had stabbed Germany in the back was voiced again and again, but it was a lie. And yet, people applauded when Hitler said it. The idea was popular and widespread. Many Germans were looking for someone to blame. Jews had often been scapegoats in the past and were easy to attack now.

This chart was used to distinguish Jews from Aryans and Germans of mixed race in order to uphold the "Law for the Protection of German Blood and Honor."

Historians have searched for many years for the moment when Hitler became a rabid anti-Semite. Hitler's own statements point to Vienna, where he first read anti-Semitic literature. But many historians believe the pivotal moment occurred in Munich. They think that the experience of the failed communist revolt was important to him. They also believe that the classes and lectures he took part in played a role. It may be that the answer is very complicated, with no precise turning point. Hate is a simple emotion; learning to hate may be very complicated.

A Great Speaker

Hitler discovered his talent as a speaker in Munich. The soldiers and others who listened to his lectures were greatly impressed. His ability to sway crowds grew quickly, until he ranked as one of the most influential speakers of all time.

Anti-Semitism was just one of Hitler's themes. It fit with his goal of making

Germany strong again. A strong Germany must not be governed by communists or Jews, he insisted. It had to be racially pure. Germans had to turn away from the weakness and corruption of Jews and others.

Hitler cited Jews as scapegoats. He blamed them for anything and everything bad. Jews were rich or Jews were vermin. Jews were capitalists or Jews were communists. Whatever Hitler wanted to denounce in a speech, he claimed it was Jewish.

From Workers to Nazis

Besides making speeches to soldiers, Hitler's duties in the army included spying on local political groups. On Friday, Sept. 12, 1919, these duties brought Hitler to a meeting of the German Workers' Party. The party was one of several groups with similar aims. All wanted Germany to return to its former glory. They were opposed to communism, though they did back some socialist ideas.

This party, however, would end up being different from the others. It took years, but it would grow larger and more powerful than any other party in the country. Eventually its name would be changed to the National Socialist German Workers' Party or NSDAP. Today, we know the Party and its followers as Nazis.

2. Revolution

Everything was in chaos in the beer hall. Members of the city and state government had come to hear a speech. Instead, the Nazis and their illegal army, the SA, had taken them prisoner. But no one seemed to know exactly what to do.

It was the fall of 1923. The German economy had sunk to a new low. Everyone was talking about revolution—the communists, the Nazis, everyone. Something had to be done. But this?

The Nazi Party was still small. Hitler was one of its leaders, but he wasn't in complete control. He even had trouble getting through the crowd with his bodyguards to meet with the officials and Nazis inside. Once there, everyone started talking at once. Hitler did not know exactly what to do. The capture of the Munich officials was supposed to be the start of a Nazi revolution against the government. That part had gone well. But there were signs that the army wasn't going along as some had promised it would.

Hitler glanced toward his supporters. They were well-armed. A heavy machine gun sat at the back of the hall. But the men were mostly unemployed former soldiers, desperate for work. Some were probably as hungry as he had been a few years before, when he begged for food at a homeless shelter. Could he and the other party leaders lead Germany to glory with only their support?

Not Much of a Party

When he first began spying on them in 1919, Hitler didn't think much of the German Workers Party. However, he agreed with much of what the Party leaders said. He also may have received support and encouragement from his army commander to join and strengthen the small party.

Hitler quickly became an important Party member. Not only could he speak very well to large groups, he was a superb organizer. Hitler remained in the army until March 1920, spending more and more time with the Party. By the time of his discharge from the army, he was one of the Party's best speakers and a key member.

Hitler wore a loose fitting suit jacket during his speeches. Usually these lasted two hours. He almost always talked of Germany's glorious past, contrasting it to the present chaos. The past he talked about was an ideal myth that hadn't actually existed, but it inspired the crowd. Hitler claimed that Jews and communists took advantage of Germans. They were the enemy. He criticized the agreement that ended the World War, which was imposing harsh conditions on Germany. And he promised a better future through nationalism and a return to old values like hard work.

As the Party grew, its organization shifted. Its name changed to the National Socialist German Workers' Party or NSDAP. It was from this abbreviation that the word "Nazi" was derived, because of the sound of the German letters. Hitler at first refused to be the Party chairman. Conflicts with others led him to quit temporarily. But suddenly he began working hard to take over. In the summer of 1921, he became chairman, or "Führer."

The Economy Crashes

At the end of World War I, the victorious allies imposed large fines or reparations on Germany. Raising money to pay them helped wreck the German economy. Even without them, the economy would have had a hard time recovering from the war. Businesses had closed. Many people lacked jobs.

A large number of the unemployed joined paramilitary organizations. These were called by many names, including the *Freikorps* or

Free Corps. Some were used by local governments to keep order. Others were sponsored by or aligned with political parties and acted like bodyguards for them. The Free Corps also used violence to support political aims. They would attack opponents, for example, or enforce a boycott. They were sometimes responsible for murder.

The Nazis had one such group of their own. They were called the *Sturmabteilung*, the SA, or storm troopers. The SA started as security officers for large meetings in the Munich beer halls. Like the other paramilitary groups, they were brutal when dealing with enemies.

By the end of 1921, the SA was headed by Ernst Röhm. Röhm remained a close friend of Hitler for the next decade. His efforts at organizing the SA were an important part of the Party's success. Like the rest of the Party, the SA slowly increased in membership.

Things in Germany went from bad to worse in the early 1920s. The government failed to deliver some of the coal and wood owed as reparations. The French decided to retaliate. In January 1923, the French army occupied the Ruhr, an industrial section of Germany near France. The German government began a campaign of passive resistance. That only made things worse. By the time the government finally gave in to the French, the economy was shattered. Prices escalated and money became worthless. Necessities like bread and milk cost millions of German marks. Life savings were wiped out. Many people wanted to overthrow the national and state governments. Revolutions and takeovers— called "putsches," from a German word for a sudden or quick thrust—occurred in many parts of the country.

Among those clamoring for a putsch were Nazi Party members in Munich. Hitler and other Nazis had been denouncing the city government for a long time. Their supporters wanted more than just criticism. They wanted action. On November 8, 1923, Hitler and the other Nazi leaders finally agreed. Several hundred SA and other party members armed themselves with machine guns and other weapons. They surrounded a beer hall where prominent members of the city and state government were listening to a speech. The Nazis took them prisoner. They declared a new "Reich," a new government for all of Germany as well as Bavaria.

Chaos

In later years, Hitler would use glowing words to describe the putsch. In reality, it was an inept bungle. Hitler couldn't make up his mind exactly what to do once the government officials were taken prisoner. His demands were muddled. His supporters like Röhm were just as disorganized. In the meantime, the army and state police remained loyal to the government. By 5 AM the next day, it was obvious that their revolution had failed.

Hitler and the Nazis decided to march to the center of the city. They may have believed that

Hitler, Göring, and others commemorate the eleventh anniversary of the 1923 Beer Hall Putsch by retracing the route of the march.

the citizens of the city would join them. Or they may have been unable to think of anything better to do. As they marched, Hitler and several other leaders at the front of the group linked their hands. There were roughly two thousand party members in the procession, many armed with guns. One group of policemen retreated as they headed in the direction of the Defense

Ministry. But the Nazis soon came up against a second, larger group of policemen blocking the street. As they approached the barricades, the police began shooting. Nazi Party members threw themselves to the ground and then ran for their lives. Among those who ran away was Adolf Hitler.

The "Drummer"

Fourteen Nazi followers and four policemen were killed in the riot that ended the Beer Hall Putsch. Many more were wounded. Hitler dislocated his arm. He was arrested at the home where he had gone to have his injury treated. The police charged him with treason.

At his trial, Hitler was allowed to talk about his political beliefs. He tried to put the German government on trial. He called himself a "drummer" for the patriotic forces in Germany. Most Germans were not Nazis, but Hitler made the Nazis sound as if they were the nation's future leaders.

Hitler confessed to his actions, but he said they could not be considered treason. Treason had been committed by the government in signing the armistice of November 1918. The "November criminals" were the ones who were guilty of treason. He spoke well. Many, including the judge, were on his side by the time the trial ended. Nonetheless, he was convicted and sentenced to five years in prison. He would end up serving less than one year.

3. The Path to Power

Hitler strode to the front of the hall, confident, ready, following behind the wedge of brown-shirted SA men. Seven thousand people had crowded into the Circus Krone auditorium in Munich. All were on their feet, cheering, yelling, screaming "Heil," and delivering Nazi salutes. Standing before the microphones, Hitler drank it in for a moment. It was 1927, and the state authorities had just lifted the ban that prevented him from making public speeches.

It was a moment of triumph. After years of hard work, he had become party Führer, the one and only leader. The Party remained small, but it was well organized, dedicated, and enthusiastic. The roar in the auditorium warmed him. He let it continue a moment longer, then took a half step forward and thrust out his hand.

"Heil!" screamed the crowd in delight. "Hail to our leader! Heil!"

The Mid-1920s: Near Oblivion

Hitler's trial helped make him a well-known figure throughout Germany. But by the time he was released from jail, the German economy had begun to improve. The Nazis, like many of the other small, fanatical parties, lost support. People didn't feel quite as desperate. Hopeful about their own futures, they didn't fall for the messages of hate. Meanwhile, the failed putsch had damaged the Nazi's reputation. They looked like inept bunglers. The putsch and Hitler's imprisonment also caused dissension and disorganization within the Party. Members left for other groups or lost interest. Leaders feuded with each other.

After he was released from jail, Hitler devoted a great deal of his time to reorganizing the Nazi movement. He did not do this alone, of course. Among those who helped him were Hermann Göring, a World War I fighter pilot who had been wounded in the putsch. Another was Gregor Strasser. With his brother Otto, Gregor played an important role in the Party, especially in Berlin. Hitler eventually split with the Strasser brothers—first with Otto, then with Gregor. The conflict was partly over political philosophy. Otto leaned more toward socialism than Hitler did. But the conflict was also about power and popularity. During the early 1920s, Hitler increased his hold over the Party. He was very good at outmaneuvering opponents and keeping underlings and allies off balance. Despite his disagreements with the Strassers, he was careful not to attack them directly while they were still powerful. Gregor remained an important party member through the 1920s. He was second only to Hitler.

Hypnotism

Hitler had a special ability when speaking to large audiences. Some people who observed it compared it to hypnotism. His voice had a strident ring to it. With sharp gestures and rising emotions, Hitler could excite a crowd. His speeches could last for hours. They tended to follow simple themes that Hitler repeated over and over again:

> *Germany had been great.*
> *Germany had been betrayed at the*
> *   end of World War I.*
> *The Jews and communists*
> *   were responsible.*

Hero Worship

Hitler was also an excellent organizer, able to inspire other people to do hard work for the Party. Hitler himself did not spend long hours at a desk or in an office. He was capable of attending to many details and had an excellent memory. Hitler was very aware that a big part of his "job" was to create a larger-than-life image of a leader. He upheld this image always.

Hitler also had a unique ability to make others feel important. People meeting him felt as if they were the center of his attention. He had tricks that helped him. One was a prolonged handshake. Another was a long stare into someone's eyes. Part of Hitler's success came from knowing what the other person expected. This indirect flattery and his personal charm were important weapons of persuasion. His temper was a powerful weapon as well.

Hitler's ideas and abilities led many people to worship him as a hero. One of the most important people who did so was Joseph Goebbels. Goebbels joined the Party around the time that Hitler was jailed. Though disabled with a club foot, Goebbels was extremely intelligent and an able speaker. He met Hitler for the first time around 1925. At

Joseph Goebbels (left), minister of propaganda for
the Nazi Party, stands next to Hitler
in a group of Nazi officers.

first, Goebbels was an ally of Gregor Strasser.
His political philosophy was nearer to
Strasser's than to Hitler's. But Hitler won him
over to his side. He did this through flattery
and by giving him important party jobs.
Goebbels, like many others, saw Hitler as a
father figure for the country. He believed that
Germany needed a strong leader and saw
Hitler as that leader.

1928: A Turn for the Worse

Hitler and the Nazis believed that democracy was a weak form of government. But the Party participated in the country's elections. Hitler stated that the Nazis would come to power legally. Some historians and biographers believe that the failed putsch taught him that armed force alone would never be enough to take power.

As hard as Hitler and others worked, the Nazis remained a small party through the mid-1920s. Like America in its Roaring Twenties, Germany was experiencing good economic times. But things were starting to change again at about the time the speaking ban was lifted on Hitler. The economy was already showing some signs of weakness. At the same time, Hitler's work at organizing the Nazis was starting to pay off.

In the May 1928 elections, the Nazi Party managed to elect twelve representatives to the country's parliament, which was called the Reichstag. Among the representatives were three very important Nazis: Göring, Goebbels, and Gregor Strasser. At first glance, the election results appeared disappointing. There were over 500 seats in the Reichstag. Many people interpreted the results as proof that the Nazis were insignificant. But the election was a sign of things to come. The Nazis' best results had come from voters who were suffering economically. Hitler and others recognized the trend. Instead of giving up, they worked harder than ever to get people to join the Party.

Depression

On August 1, 1929, somewhere between thirty and forty thousand Nazi Party members, many of them members of the SA, descended on Nuremberg. For four days, they filled the town and the stadium there with chants and slogans. The Nazi swastika was plastered everywhere. Hitler presided over it all, with carefully planned public appearances. Behind the scenes, small groups of Party leaders and organizers took their cue from him, laying out plans for the near future. It was now clear to everyone that the economy was turning sour. France and Britain were pushing for more reparations.

Soon after the Party congress, the American stock market crashed. The crash was the final blow to the world economy. It had a sharp effect on Germany, because the country had been using American loans to help keep things going. When those loans dried up, things in Germany got even worse.

Hitler exploited these bad times. He attacked the reparation plan. He repeated his message that the Nazis could save Germany. In some instances, he seems to have softened his attacks on Jews, though he continued to use what we might call code words like "vermin" and "disease." Still, it was pretty clear that he and many other Nazis were anti-Semitic.

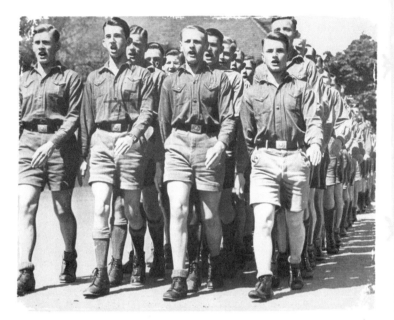

Boys marching in formation at one of Hitler's
Nazi youth camps

The Party did well in state elections in 1929.
In some cases, the votes it won in local
elections doubled. More importantly, many
young people joined the Party. Their energy
helped increase the Party's efforts.

There were two main reasons why many
people looked to the Nazis during hard times.
First, they provided both a scapegoat and a
solution—the Jews were the cause of the

problem, and getting rid of them would lead to a grand future. Some people also saw the Nazis as a counterweight to the communists. Hitler's rhetoric was strongly anticommunist. Nazi SA members often fought Communist Party members in the streets. They appeared to be the communists' natural enemies.

The Election of 1930

Hitler appointed Goebbels to organize the Party's campaign during the summer of 1930. It proved to be a brilliant stroke. Goebbels, who had headed the Party in Berlin, was a master campaign manager. He organized speeches and Party meetings all across the country. Handouts and newspapers were used to spread propaganda. Goebbels orchestrated SA demonstrations, fights, and riots to gain the Party publicity.

Hitler gave speeches all across the country during the campaign's final weeks. He sensed that the Party would do well. At one point he

Chancellor Hitler (standing) opens the German parliament, the Reichstag.

predicted that the Nazis would come to power by 1934. But probably not even Hitler could have predicted the outcome of the election. Instead of the twelve seats they had held, the Nazis ended up with 107. Approximately 6.5 million Germans had voted for the Nazis, making them the second largest party in the Reichstag. The Nazis, and Hitler, had arrived.

4. The Deal

Hitler was exhausted, dead tired from weeks of campaigning for president. He had given speech after speech around the clock from the beginning of 1932, and it was now April. For the past few days he had flown from one city to another all over the country. All in a race no one thought he could win.

It was Goebbels' fault. The Nazi campaign manager was pushing harder than ever. But Goebbels was a genius. Germany had never seen a campaign like this. And Hitler, who had seemed like a long-shot, actually had a chance of doing well. The National Socialists were creating a sensation.

Hitler's fatigue began to melt as he walked in the direction of the podium. The crowd began

This presidential election poster reads
"Enough now! Elect Hitler"

shouting, and instantly he felt energized. In short order, he had the audience on its feet. "It is time for the old man, Hindenburg, to step aside," he said, repeating a theme he had used at every stop. Again and again he said a new leader would come from the "Volk," the German people. And he, Adolf Hitler, was that leader.

To Run or Not?

Hitler hadn't been able to decide whether to run for president of Germany or not. Everyone knew that Paul von Hindenburg, the former field marshall and incumbent president, would win. But the Nazis' impressive victories during the recent Reichstag elections made it important for them to challenge Hindenburg. If they didn't, their gains might be lost.

On the other hand, if the candidate lost badly, they'd be finished. The only person in the Party well known enough to challenge Hindenburg was Hitler. But it was a very risky move. Goebbels and other important Nazis convinced Hitler it was worth the gamble. While Hindenburg was very popular, many candidates were running for president. They would divide up the votes. Hitler's supporters, however, were likely to remain loyal. That would give him a strong base. Not enough to win, maybe, but enough to finish strongly. He might even force a runoff or second election. It would make Hitler look like an important leader.

Goebbels was right. When the votes were counted, Hitler finished second with roughly 30 percent of the vote. This helped force a second election with only three candidates. Besides Hitler and Hindenburg, there was a third candidate, Ernst Thalmann, a communist.

A Strong Second

Campaigning in the runoff election was even more furious. Hitler delivered twenty speeches in roughly a week's time. Goebbels and thousands of other Party leaders, speakers, and members worked just as hard.

As expected, Hitler lost to Hindenburg in the runoff election. But he polled 37 percent of the vote. This was more than had been predicted. Over a third of the German electorate had now voted for Hitler and his party at least once. But the hard work and campaigning of 1932 was just beginning. After the presidential election, local and state elections were held in late April. That meant another round of fierce campaigning. Again, Hitler flew all over the country. Again, the Nazis did well. The Party waited for new Reichstag elections set for the end of July.

Personal Life

Hitler was now in his forties. His book, *Mein Kampf,* was a best-seller. Speaking fees also gave him plenty of money, though personal wealth did not seem to be his goal. His primary concern was politics, power, and the Nazi Party. He had some other interests, like architecture, but no real hobbies or outside interests.

While Hitler liked being with women, there is little evidence that he had any love affairs until after World War I. And the few relationships he had with women during the 1920s and early 1930s seem to have been superficial. There was one exception—Geli Raubal. Geli was the daughter of Hitler's half-sister, Angela Raubal. They met during the summer of 1925, when Hitler was staying at a house in Berchtesgarten in the Bavarian Alps. At the time, Geli was seventeen. In 1929, she moved to his apartment in Munich.

While Hitler seems to have been emotionally attached to Geli, historians are not sure their relationship was sexual. Geli flirted openly with other men and may have had an affair with Hitler's chauffeur. Hitler gradually became jealous and more controlling. By the fall of 1931, Geli wanted to leave Hitler. The reason is unclear. She may have found a new boyfriend, or she may have simply wanted to be out of her uncle's control. Whatever the case, she was clearly unhappy with their relationship.

On September 18, 1931, Hitler left Munich for Nuremberg. The next morning he received word that Geli had been found dead in his apartment, his pistol by her side. The death was declared a suicide, though that didn't stop all sorts of rumors from spreading.

The German Government

After World War I, Germany was run by a president, a chancellor, and a parliament called the Reichstag. An absolute majority could select the chancellor. The chancellor would then select ministers who would run the government. Whichever party controlled the Reichstag would select its leader as chancellor. But Germany had many parties in the Reichstag. None of them alone could get a majority. They had to compromise and work together. As time went on, differences in political philosophy and personality clashes made compromise impossible.

At the same time, the president of Germany had unusual power, both because of the constitution and, in the case of Hindenburg, his personal prestige. Under the constitution, he could allow a chancellor to form a government without approval from the Reichstag. In other words, the president could say it was okay for a chancellor to rule without agreement in the Reichstag. Hindenburg did this several times. He did it so often that it became the common way for the government to function. This divided the government and left the chancellor weak. It also distanced the public from the government.

The system worked until the economic problems of the late 1920s and early 1930s. Then the lack of cooperation between the parties made it impossible to agree on solutions. These disputes also meant that an unusual number of Reichstag elections had to be held. Dissolving the government and calling for new elections was one way to try and find a majority. But it ended up helping the Nazis.

The Biggest Party

The July 1932 Reichstag elections were a great victory for the Nazis. They won 230 seats. They were now the largest party in the Reichstag. But the victory proved frustrating. They weren't large enough to select a chancellor on their own. And they couldn't find another party to work with.

Hindenburg and the others refused to make Hitler chancellor. They didn't want him to head the government. Hitler refused compromises that would have given him or other Party members less important roles in the cabinet. He wanted to be number one, or he didn't want to be involved. He thought Hindenburg would give in. He was wrong. A new government was formed without the Nazis—and then dissolved. Hitler felt defeated. He had failed to achieve the powerful position in government that he wanted.

A New Election

In the fall elections, the Nazi Party didn't do quite as well as it had during the summer. Hitler's party got about 33 percent of the vote, but lost more than thirty seats. Still, they were the biggest party in the Reichstag, with 196 representatives. Again, no party had an absolute majority. Again, no coalition could be formed. And once again, the president stepped in to choose a chancellor.

Hitler continued to maneuver. He tried to convince Hindenburg to select him. He offered to accept cabinet members from outside the Nazi Party. But Hindenburg held firm against him. He appointed Kurt von Schleicher chancellor.

Schleicher tried to split the Nazis by getting Gregor Strasser to take the position of vice chancellor. Hitler reacted quickly, calling on subordinates and personally speaking to Party members across the country to cement his support. He asserted himself with diplomacy and skill, using all of his talents as an organizer and a persuader. Strasser quickly realized he was in no position to challenge Hitler and resigned from the Party.

Schleicher soon lost Hindenburg's support. The president began looking for a new chancellor. At first, he favored naming a past chancellor, Franz von Papen. Papen was an aristocrat with important family and business connections. He was a centrist politician, though he had split with other members of his party, the Center Party. But it soon became clear that Papen couldn't get enough support.

Papen then put together a deal to have Hitler named chancellor, with himself vice chancellor. Nazis would have only a limited number of seats in the new cabinet. One key to the deal was an alliance between the conservative German National Party and the Nazis, which Papen managed to arrange.

Historians have debated why Hindenburg agreed to the deal. Some point out that Hitler

Hitler greets President Hindenburg at the ceremonies in Postdam.

and the Nazis seemed weakened by the November election. Some feel this meant that Hindenburg should have ignored Hitler. Others think Hindenburg had less reason to fear Hitler. A few believe that Hitler and the Nazis had found embarrassing information about a land deal and were blackmailing Hindenburg. Others say that Hindenburg, who had been born in 1847 and was now in his eighties, was senile and simply gave in to the arguments of people he trusted, including his son.

Whatever Hindenburg's reasons, the Nazis had strong support throughout the country. At the same time, German leaders like Papen clearly underestimated Hitler. They may not have taken him or his movement seriously. Papen told other conservatives that he would "push Hitler into a corner," according to historian Henry Ashby Turner. Hitler's hateful ideas about Jews and his attacks against democracy were clearly expressed in his speeches. The history of the Nazi Party demonstrated that Hitler would not hesitate to use violence to reach his goals. If anyone in the country didn't believe he would try to put these ideas into practice, they were very, very mistaken.

"Forward with God!"

Schleicher was forced to resign as chancellor on January 28, 1933. On the night of January 29,

Hitler gathered with Göring and other Party
leaders at Goebbels' house in Berlin. He had
concluded the deal with Papen, but the army's
opinion was unknown. The final lineup of the
cabinet wasn't set. Hitler spent a sleepless night,
worrying about what might go wrong. But he
didn't have to worry. The next morning, Hitler,
Göring and other Nazis joined Papen and
other conservative politicians at the Reich
Chancellery. They argued in the room outside
the president's office over some last minute
details, but in the end, Hitler was shown in to
the president and was sworn in.

"Forward with God," said Hindenburg.

5. Long Knives and Paradoxes

Hitler stomped down the hall, sweeping into the small hotel room. Ernst Röhm, the head of the SA, lay sleeping in the bed. At least he was alone. There had been rumors he wouldn't be, and that his "guest" would be male.

"Röhm, you're under arrest," thundered Hitler. He snapped his rhino-hide riding crop against his leg. Röhm, half asleep, tried to ask Hitler what was going on.

"You're under arrest!" shouted the Führer, spinning on his heel and leaving Röhm to the officers he'd brought with him on this hot summer night. It was the last time he would see his former friend alive.

A Threat from Within

Hitler arrested Röhm on Saturday, June 30, 1934. It was part of a crackdown against the SA. Many men besides Röhm, perhaps as many as 400, were murdered. The action removed the greatest threat to Hitler's control of the country. Ironically, that threat came from some of his closest supporters and oldest friends—the illegal army that had helped bring him to power.

The SA had grown in power along with Hitler. It had increased in size and was well-armed. It had set up concentration camps to punish its enemies. These were the precursors of the death camps used later to exterminate Jews and others. With its size and power growing, Nazi leaders realized that the SA might someday be strong enough to overthrow the government. They were also seen by the army as a serious threat. Hitler needed the army's backing to govern, so this presented continual problems.

For months, Hitler debated how to deal
with Röhm. Some steps were taken. Control of
the concentration camps was eventually taken
away from the SA leadership. But Hitler's fear
that the SA would turn against him grew. There
were rumors that a putsch or coup was being
planned. Many SA members were angry that
the German economy had not improved fast
enough. Röhm had been with Hitler from the

Group portrait of a Nazi SA unit

early days of the struggle. Hitler liked him and
felt loyal to him. And with perhaps hundreds
of thousands of men ready to follow him,
curbing Röhm was a delicate matter.

A Legal Dictator

It may seem odd that the greatest threat to
Hitler's power was from his friends. But by the
summer of 1934, Hitler had managed to
eliminate or outmaneuver his other
opponents. The Nazi leader had increased his
hold on power in several ways. Sometimes he
used intimidation and threats. Often, however,
his methods were democratic and at least
technically legal.

Immediately after he came to power in
1933, the Reichstag burned. Hitler and others
claimed that the fire was set as part of a
communist conspiracy. They then used the fire
as an excuse to ban the communists and some
other left-wing members from the Reichstag.
With them out, the Nazis voted themselves

more power. The law giving Hitler expanded power was called the "Enabling Act." This law helped make Hitler a legal dictator.

The Nazis threatened legislators and pressured them to vote for the act. Many representatives felt they were bullied into supporting it. Even so, the law and Hitler were popular with the people.

As time went on, there was less and less opposition in the Reichstag. In some cases, parties that might have opposed the Nazis were either banned or intimidated. In other cases, interest in those parties dwindled due to the Nazis' popularity. Communists were persecuted. Some were imprisoned; a few were killed. Many wisely fled for their lives.

Other Means to Power

Hitler also gained more control of the government and police by moving Party members into important positions. Since he had absolute control of the Party, he could exert his control through Party members. His popularity also helped tremendously. Many people, even those who didn't vote for him, liked Hitler and wanted him to succeed. As Hindenburg grew older and sicker, his influence gradually decreased. In some ways, President Hindenburg had been a check on the Nazis. The less important he was, the more important Hitler became.

Finally, Hitler won support from the army. Some historians believe that he may have agreed to curb the SA in exchange for this backing. The evidence is unclear, however.

The Threat

Hitler had reason to fear Röhm and the SA. Many storm troopers seemed to be disillusioned or disappointed in the Party. The SA had included the most violent and radical members of the Party. Many of them worried that the Nazi leadership was moving too slowly.

Prodded by Nazi leaders like Himmler and Göring, Hitler finally decided to act. He may have believed false documents that indicated the SA was planning a coup. Or he may have known the documents were fake. In any event, he worked himself into a rage on the weekend of June 29 to July 1, 1934 and supervised the arrests. Some other political enemies, including Gregor Strasser, were killed in the purge.

Control and Support

When Hindenburg died in August 1934, Hitler took over as president as well as chancellor. He had achieved his goal; he was absolute dictator. He was also extremely popular. Today, we think of dictators as harsh leaders whom everyone hates. But Hitler was actually loved by many people.

How could a dictator be popular? For one thing, Hitler avoided the conflicts that had crippled earlier German governments. Most members of the Party worked together. His dictatorial ways brought order to the government. The improving economy was a more important reason. The entire world, including Germany, was in a major depression. Many people were without jobs. Wages remained low and food prices high. But Hitler's government made things better. People felt optimistic about the future.

Nazi propaganda, organized by Goebbels, was another reason. It always showed Hitler in the best light. And Hitler stood up to England and France. Many people felt that the two nations were trying to bully Germany. By reinstating the draft and disregarding the Versailles treaty, Hitler told the two allies that Germany would not be pushed around. This made Germans feel good about themselves and their country. Millions joined the Nazi Party.

Hitler Against Jews

Once in power, the Nazis took several steps against Jews. On April 1, 1933, Goebbels and

other Nazis organized a boycott of Jewish
businesses. It was a failure. Many Germans
simply ignored it; others complained about SA
violence against Jews. The boycott quickly
ended, but anti-Semitic propaganda and
persecution continued. Jews were beaten on
the street. Laws were passed greatly restricting
Jewish life.

A German civilian wearing a Nazi armband holds
anti-Jewish boycott signs, while SA members
paste them onto the storefronts of
Jewish-owned businesses.

In 1935, the Nazi-controlled Reichstag instituted the Nuremberg Laws. The most important of these laws stripped Jews of their legal rights as citizens. Basically, the law declared that Jews were enemies of Germany. It provided "legal" grounds not only to discriminate against Jews, but to take their property—and their lives. Roughly a quarter of the Jewish population left Germany between 1933 and 1937. And then things got even worse.

In the fall of 1938, high-ranking Nazis organized a countrywide "action" against Jews. Assaults against Jews and their property were carefully planned. Stores were smashed and many Jewish people were arrested and taken to concentration camps. The action became known as *Kristallnacht,* Crystal Night, or the Night of Broken Glass. *Kristallnacht* and the Nuremberg Laws made it clear that Hitler was serious about making Germany "pure." More Jews fled Germany after *Kristallnacht.* But it soon became very difficult for them to do so.

Today, historians debate exactly how anti-Semitic Germans were when Hitler came to power. Some believe that pressures from radical SA members and other Nazis led to the Nuremberg Laws. They point out that Hitler sometimes toned down his attacks. They remind us that others besides Hitler shared the blame for the violence against Jews.

SA members hold hands on the steps of the University of Vienna in an attempt to prevent Jews from entering the building.

Still, it is clear that Hitler saw Jews as a cancer that had to be removed from Germany. Widespread violence against Jews could not have continued without his approval.

Living Space

Besides purifying the German race, Hitler had another major goal—restoring the borders of "Greater Germany" and then adding "living space" in the east. This meant taking over Austria and parts of other countries where ethnic Germans lived. It also meant invading countries to the east like Poland and the Soviet Union and using them as colonies.

He began working towards this goal by expanding the military. This was a violation of the Versailles treaty. Hitler went even further in March 1936, when he marched troops into the Rhineland. Though this was German territory, it bordered France. Placing troops in this area was forbidden by the treaty. Though his army was still weak, Hitler gambled that the French would do nothing. He was right. "Had the French marched into the Rhineland," he later said, "we would have had to withdraw." It set the stage for annexing Austria and Czechoslovakia.

Greater Germany

Like Hitler, many Austrians considered themselves Germans rather than Austrians. But Austria included many people who were not ethnic Germans. And even many of those who were German did not want to unite with Germany. Hitler encouraged Austrian Nazis to campaign for annexation. He worked diplomatically to bring the countries together. He also threatened Austria with his army. As the Austrian government resisted, he stepped up pressure. Finally, in early 1938, he ordered German troops to prepare an invasion. There was a great deal of pressure on the Austrians. Not only was there a large German army on their border, but many Austrians were demonstrating in favor of the Nazis. Finally, the government complied.

On March 12, 1938, Hitler crossed the Austrian border to visit his birthplace at Braunau. Victory made him bolder. Within a month and a half, he mapped out a plan for similar action against Czechoslovakia. This time, Great Britain and France tried to stop Hitler. They seemed ready to go to war. Hitler felt it was a bluff, but his generals didn't. They may even have planned to overthrow Hitler if war started. But if so, they never got the chance. As Hitler had calculated, Great Britain and France were not prepared to go to war against Germany over Czechoslovakia. They reached an agreement that gave part of the country to Germany without a fight. British Prime Minister Neville Chamberlain declared that the negotiations had guaranteed "peace in our time." In reality, this weakness only made Hitler bolder.

6. Military Conquest

The hot July sun beat down through the trees of Versailles as Hitler's car halted. The Führer emerged from the Mercedes limousine. He wore a military uniform with his Iron Cross pinned proudly to his chest. Slowly, he walked through the thick shade of the trees to a railroad car on an old siding. The railroad car had been the scene of Germany's humiliating surrender at the end of World War I.

Hitler surveyed the scene with a deep smile. His armies had conquered France a few weeks before. It was one of the great military victories of all time. He climbed atop the granite block the French had placed to commemorate the end of World War I. Hands on hips, he glanced

German soldiers parade in Warsaw to celebrate the
conquest of Poland.

around contemptuously. The great stain of
Versailles, the shame of the November
criminals, had finally been erased.

France Falls

Germany began World War II with an invasion
of Poland in September 1939. German
airplanes, tanks, and soldiers swept quickly

into the country. A new word was invented to describe the quickness of the attack: "blitzkrieg," or lightning war.

The steps leading to the invasion were similar to those Hitler had used against Austria and Czechoslovakia. But this time Great Britain and France declared war on Germany. They had finally decided to take Hitler seriously. Even so, the French and British armies took little action against the Germans at first. Within a month, Germany controlled most of Poland. The Soviet Union invaded eastern Poland at the same time. The Soviets had a secret agreement with the Germans to split the country.

Hitler's invasion of Poland was extremely popular in Germany. Many Germans felt it was rightfully theirs. The conquest also brought riches to many Germans. They were able to set up businesses in the occupied territory and make a great deal of money. But above all, the easy victories in Austria, Czechoslovakia, and Poland made Hitler

Two German sentries stand guard in front of a gate
marking the border between Soviet-
and German-occupied Poland.

popular because they were just that—easy
victories. Few Germans had been killed. At
the same time, German territory had been
greatly expanded.

On May 10, 1940, Hitler's armies
began sweeping through Denmark, the
Netherlands, Belgium, Holland, and France.
Eighty-nine divisions, including ten Panzer

or tank divisions, led the charge. Relying on better weapons and training as well as surprise, the Germans moved quickly. By June 14, Paris had fallen. France surrendered a few days later.

The army made plans to invade Great Britain. The German Luftwaffe, or air force, launched a massive bombing campaign against England. Civilian as well as military targets were hit. But Hitler's chief aim remained the one he had proclaimed years before in *Mein Kampf*: living space in the East. That meant Russia. As the idea of invading England faded, the army began moving its troops eastward.

Hitler as a General

Hitler had been a corporal in World War I. While that gave him a lot of practical experience, it did not train him to lead armies. Nor had he studied strategy or tactics. But he played an important role in leading the German military. Besides setting general policy, he understood new weapons and military technology. He made sure the army generals had new weapons and pushed them to use these weapons effectively. German tanks and large artillery pieces were developed on his direct orders. As the war went on, he influenced and directed battle strategy and tactics.

Historians have debated how good a general Hitler was. His abilities are difficult to assess, however, since the army won great victories and suffered terrible defeats because of his decisions. It is clear, however, that he considered his role as military commander part of his job as Führer. He believed that his political goals called for military victory. He also believed that he was the only one who could achieve them. While this made him bold as a general, it also made him stubborn. He was unwilling to retreat at times when it would have been wise to do so.

The USSR and Einsatzgruppen

In the dawn of June 22, 1941, German troops launched an attack on the Soviet Union. They were the spearhead of a massive army numbering over a million men, with more than 3,500 tanks and 2,700 airplanes. It was the largest army ever assembled. For several weeks, the German troops were as successful as any army in history. By November, they stood fifty miles from the gates of Moscow, the Soviet capital.

But as the cold gray skies of Russia began to fill with snowflakes, the German advance stalled. The change in the weather signaled a change in German fortunes. The army was not properly equipped or trained for winter battle. More importantly, the army faced a massive enemy. Despite the Russians' early losses, their army was well-motivated. The soldiers were protecting their homes and families. The Russian population was larger than the

German population. Once the Soviet army could be reorganized and supplied, it would be a powerful force. But this lay ahead. In the fall of 1941, the German army consolidated its victories. The Germans dug in and made defensive posts as the winter came on.

Another group of Germans were busy behind the lines. Special units known as *Einsatzgruppen* had followed the army into Russia. Directed by the SS (*Schutzstaffel*, the guard unit of the Nazi Party). and the Gestapo, these groups were actually death squads. Their targets were Soviet officials and Communist Party members in the occupied territory, and Jews. As living space was acquired, Hitler's other great goal—ridding Europe of Jews—would also be achieved.

7. The Holocaust

As Joseph Goebbels returned to his office on an early December evening in 1941, he glanced up at the painting on the wall. Emperor Frederick II glared down imperiously. The emperor had done great things for the German people, Goebbels thought, but not nearly as much as his own beloved Führer, Adolf Hitler. Goebbels loved the Führer with his whole being.

He especially approved of Hitler's latest action. Goebbels himself had been pushing for it for many years. Goebbels sat at the desk and began to dictate his diary entry. He had been keeping the journal for years, recording his thoughts on politics, Germany, and Hitler. All of the great events of the Nazi Party were recorded there. There was nothing different or special about today's entry. It was a matter of simple fact:

The Führer has decided to make a clean sweep. He told the Jews that if they again brought about a world war, they would be annihilated. That wasn't a slogan. The war is here.

Hitler never wrote down his thoughts about the Holocaust and how it should be carried out. He usually did not issue orders on paper. He spoke to his underlings and expected them to carry out his orders. There are many records and much evidence relating to the actual murders themselves. But the decision-making process that led to them remains unclear.

Among the questions historians have is when the decision to murder the Jews was made. Did it evolve slowly? Did Hitler and others plan it from the first day they took power?

Many historians today think that the plan to murder millions of Jews evolved over the years. They point out that while Hitler and the Nazis were anti-Semitic from the very beginning, organized mass murder did not start until the invasion of Russia. Other historians point out that many Jews were killed before that. During the last months of 1941 and the early months of 1942, actions against Jews became more severe. It was only then that mass deportations and exterminations began, so many historians believe that the decision to approve mass murder happened then.

But if Hitler had always wanted to eliminate the Jews from Europe, why did he wait until the end of 1941 or the beginning of 1942? There are several possible answers. One is that while Hitler wanted to eliminate all Jews, he didn't have a chance to do so until then.

It is also possible that Hitler and the other important Nazis waited until they felt the

A street in Krakow, Poland, after the liquidation of the ghetto, is strewn with the belongings of deported Jews.

public would not protest—a euthanasia program that the Nazis had tried earlier to kill the mentally ill had been strongly criticized. Hitler may have decided to act because he was worried the war would turn against Germany. Or he may have thought the war was going so well that it was time to act against the Jews.

Nothing in Writing

The lack of a document from Hitler has led some to speculate that he was not actually involved in the Final Solution. But it is ludicrous to believe that the Holocaust could have started and continued without his approval.

Goebbels' diary entry is only one of the proofs that Hitler ordered the Holocaust. Historians have notes from Heinrich Himmler, the head of the SS, from around the same time. Historians also know when certain meetings about the Final Solution took place, and when Hitler was visited by people involved in the murders. We probably will never know all the details about Hitler's decision. We only know what happened: millions of Jews were rounded up and shipped to death camps.

Hitler's Guilt

It's not easy to kill eight million people. The *Einsatzgruppen* worked mostly with machine

Deportation of Jews from Polish ghettos

guns and some special gas vans. While they
killed thousands upon thousands of people, it
was soon clear how difficult mass executions
were going to be. Killing millions required an
assembly line of death. Jews had to be
collected in ghettos and concentration camps.
Railroads needed to be made available for
transport. New methods of killing had to be
perfected. Corpses had to be disposed of.

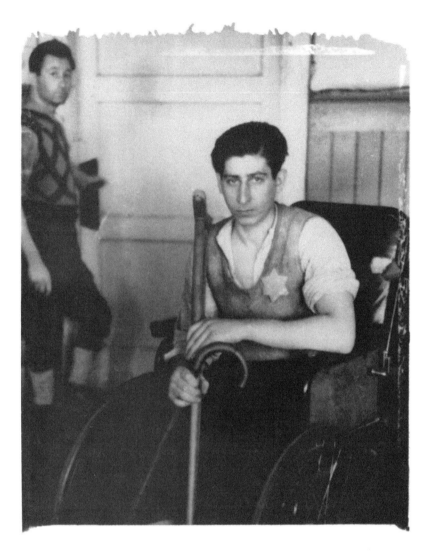

A disabled youth in the Kovno ghetto wears the
Star of David.

Thousands of Germans and other Europeans were involved in the Holocaust. Not all were Nazis. Historians have recently begun to reexamine what ordinary people did during the Holocaust. While some helped save Jews, many did not. Even before Jews were shipped en masse to their deaths, they were persecuted in Germany. They had to wear badges that showed they were Jews. They worked as slaves for the war effort. They had no rights and were robbed of property. Few non-Jewish Germans protested these measures.

That does not lessen Hitler's responsibility. Hitler raged against Jews in his first political speeches. He was the dictator of the country. He was the director and catalyst of the Holocaust. He created the atmosphere and the mechanism for death. He made it happen.

8. The End of the Thousand Year Reich

The generals arriving at Hitler's command bunker at Berchtesgarten in the German Alps wore serious, worried looks. The Americans and British had landed in France earlier in the month. Already they were threatening to break through the defenses. Paris was in danger. The German forces were worn down. Even Field Marshall Erwin Rommel, the national hero who had won great victories earlier, feared the war would be lost. On the Eastern Front, things were even worse. The Soviet army had broken through the middle of the German lines. The way to Berlin was open.

The generals had been called together to discuss the situation in Hitler's underground command center. Caverns and tunnels gave way to large rooms here. Hitler's private quarters had been drilled into solid rock. The Führer's mood was as dark and deep as the rocks. He listened to the hints that the German army should retreat, and perhaps surrender. Coldly, he told the generals Germany would not give up. Then he launched into a long speech about special weapons being developed. Pilotless bombs would drop from the sky. Speedy jet fighters would swarm overhead. Hitler shouted that the failures of his generals at the front would be overcome. The Reich would survive. The generals listened in disbelief.

Hitler's Decline

The secret weapons that Hitler talked about did exist. But the situation was far worse than he admitted, at least to his generals. Germany was on the brink of losing the war.

Meanwhile, Hitler's own health was deteriorating. It is difficult to know now whether this was due to the pressures of the war or a medical condition. Historians say that Hitler's doctor was a quack. He treated him for real and imagined ailments with drugs that were either useless or harmful. Historian H. R. Trevor-Roper says that the drugs included strychnine and belladonna, powerful poisons. There were also narcotics and stimulants. Though in his mid-fifties, Hitler looked much older. His left arm and leg trembled at times. He also had severe stomach cramps and gas.

As Hitler's health suffered, so did the German army. The Western Allies were pushing Germany back from the Mediterranean, France, and Russia. Military analysts usually call Hitler's decision to invade the Soviet Union his key blunder of the war. The vast country and its harsh weather made it difficult to conquer. On the other hand, the German army had defeated Russian armies during World War I. Because of that history and Hitler's aim of acquiring living space in the East, his attack against the Soviet Union would have seemed logical to him.

The Eastern Front slowly drained the German armies. Hitler often commanded his generals to hold ground at all cost. Even when they were successful, they suffered massive losses. The Germans suffered on other fronts, but the steady attack by the Red Army from late 1941 onward set the stage for Germany's defeat. Besides the men and materials lost there, the action against Russia drained energy and attention from other areas.

The American and British invasion of France in June 1944 sealed Germany's fate. A massive counterattack planned by Hitler that December won only a brief respite. As the winter began to give way to spring, troops closed in on Berlin from all directions.

An Attempt on His Life

As the war went badly, Hitler and other Nazis punished dissent. Penalties were increased by transferring cases to Nazi Party courts. Anyone important who disagreed publicly with Hitler's policies risked prison or worse. A state official named Theodor Korselt who suggested that Hitler step down was sentenced to death.

Most people kept silent, but the support Hitler had enjoyed in the 1930s had eroded. Several generals who attended the conferences at Hitler's headquarters wanted to overthrow the Führer. They realized Hitler wouldn't surrender and feared total annihilation. The only solution was to remove him.

Several attempts had been made to kill Hitler. According to biographer Joachim C. Fest, a time bomb had been placed on his plane in 1943 but failed to go off. Other plots had either been poorly planned or hampered by bad luck. In no case was a serious, coordinated coup carried out.

With the war going badly, some German generals and other officers decided to kill Hitler. They hoped that after Hitler was killed, others would join them. They plotted to kill the Führer and take over the government. Then they would make peace with the Western Allies.

Hitler and Italian dictator Benito Mussolini (left) inspect the wreckage of a conference room in Hitler's headquarters following a failed bombing assassination attempt.

In mid-July, Hitler traveled to his headquarters in East Prussia. Colonel Claus Schenk Stauffenberg attended a conference there on July 20. Hitler and two dozen officers were gathered in a room around a large, oak table when Stauffenberg entered. He put down his briefcase and then quickly left, pretending he had to make a phone call. A few minutes later, the briefcase exploded. The walls and ceiling crashed in. Hitler was burned and his arm paralyzed. His back was injured by a beam and his ears harmed by the explosion. But he survived. Calmly, he gave orders to arrest the conspirators.

Stauffenberg and others who had helped him were quickly captured. The conspirators had planned to use army units stationed in Berlin to take over the city. Their putsch was quickly and easily overcome. Hitler moved swiftly against the officers and civilians who had been involved in the plot. Just under 5,000 people were executed. Thousands of others were sent to concentration camps or punished in other ways. Many were actually unconnected with the attempt, but Hitler and other Nazis used it as an excuse to remove enemies.

General Rommel had spoken with the conspirators before the bomb attack. It is possible that he would have joined the putsch. However, he had been injured in an Allied

Hitler shakes hands with Rommel, the famous German general who was later linked to an attempt to assassinate the Führer.

attack a few days before. He was in the hospital when the bomb went off.

Hitler gave him a choice: stand trial or commit suicide. If he committed suicide, his family would be saved. Rommel chose suicide. Hitler honored his side of the bargain. Rommel had done him a great favor. He did not have to admit that the country's most popular general had turned against him.

Death Marches

The Holocaust continued despite the German losses. As the Russians threatened to overrun the death camps in Poland and eastern Europe, SS troops dismantled them. Orders were given to hide the evidence of the mass murders. Jews were taken from occupied countries and shipped to death centers to be exterminated even as Germany collapsed. When camps were too close to the front, Jews there were marched further east, many of them dying.

It is impossible to know exactly how many Jews and others were killed. Estimates of Jewish deaths range from 4.5 million to 8 million. By any count, the crime was immense.

No Surrender

Surrender was impossible for Hitler. It would mean utter defeat for him and his "vision" of Germany. Despite the continued losses, he kept fighting. He knew that secret weapons were being developed. He saw that the Western and Eastern Allies were divided. He remembered that he had won great victories before when all seemed lost. He also believed that Germany had lost World War I only because its leaders had given up. It is impossible to say whether he truly believed that things would turn around. At some points toward the end of the war, he seems not to have understood how badly things were going. At other times he clearly did.

Hitler knew the Allies would never accept any deal that kept him in power. They were likely to execute him if they captured him. So he felt that he personally had only two options: somehow win the war or commit suicide.

The Berlin Bunker

An underground headquarters had been built beneath the Chancellery building in Berlin. As the Allies closed in during the early months of 1945, Hitler retreated there with a few friends and government officials. Military planning continued in the bunker. But it had less and less to do with reality. Hitler's orders were often obsolete before they were issued. He celebrated his fifty-sixth birthday below ground, his mood dark and his health shattered.

Among those in the bunker with him was Eva Braun. Eva had been his companion and mistress since at least 1933. As the Russians closed in, Hitler urged Eva to leave Berlin.

She told him she would not. Her place, she said, was by his side. A witness said Hitler cried, overcome by her devotion. Around midnight on April 28, 1945, he married her.

Last Will and Testament

The next day, Hitler worked as usual. He stopped for lunch around 2 PM. Then he and Eva shook hands with all who were left in the bunker. Together, they went into their private apartment.

Hitler and Eva Braun

Both bit cyanide tablets. At the same time, Hitler pushed his 7.65 mm Walther pistol into his mouth and pulled the trigger. After the shot was heard, an aide entered the suite and found both Hitler and Eva dead. Their corpses were carried upstairs to the garden and laid down. Gasoline was poured on them. As Hitler's last followers began to pay their respects, Russian artillery shells began to rain down. They retreated back to the shelter as the bodies began to burn.

When the fire was out, the wind scattered the ashes. Aides managed to sweep the small amount left into a shell hole. The ashes were covered with earth. Hitler was no more.

In his will, Hitler showed no remorse. He spoke again of his hatred for Jews, and willed it to his people as his everlasting gift. "I call upon the leaders of the nation and all followers," he said, "to oppose the poisoner of all races, international Jewry."

Murdering millions of innocent people was an enormous crime against humanity. It made

Hitler a unique individual, one whom others have to consider and study. Many books and articles have been written as part of that study. Most are based on a careful examination of the facts. A few, however, distort the truth to put forward a special interpretation. Some writers deny that the Holocaust took place. More than fifty years after the Holocaust occurred, it is still possible to convince naïve people that Hitler has been slandered.

We may also be tempted to think that Hitler was so unique and so evil that he wasn't human. We may think that, because Hitler's crime was so special, it can't happen again. But of course that is not true. We may also mistakenly think that Hitler's evil was obvious. But it wasn't. Many people believed the things that he said about Jews. They had heard them since they were children. In the context of his times, Hitler's prejudice seemed normal and logical.

We understand this now. Hate is a powerful force, and it takes considerable vigilance and energy to expose and fight it.

Timeline

1889	April 20, Adolf Hitler is born in Austria, near the German border.
1903	Hitler's father Alois dies in January.
1907	Hitler leaves his small-town home to travel to Vienna, the capital of Austria. There he hopes to study to be an artist. He fails the entrance exam, but doesn't tell his family. Hitler's mother dies in December.
1909–1914	Hitler hits rock bottom in Vienna. Without work or money, he finds his way to a homeless shelter. Soon, however, he begins eking out a living selling paintings. In 1913, he leaves Austria for Germany after receiving his inheritance.
1914–1918	World War I. Hitler serves with the German army. He wins two medals for bravery.

1919

Hitler is still in the army after the war ends. Assigned by his commander to spy on subversive groups, he attends a National Socialist meeting. He soon joins the group. In a letter to a friend, he writes that Jews must ultimately be removed from Europe.

1920–1923

Hitler quickly becomes one of the most important Nazi speakers and a party leader.

1923

Hitler leads the Beer Hall Putsch, a disorganized attempt to take over the Munich government. Injured, he is arrested and placed on trial.

1924

Released after serving six months of his sentence, Hitler completes *Mein Kampf* and rebuilds the Nazi Party.

1929

The worldwide economic depression hits Germany hard. The downturn helps the tiny Nazi Party rise to prominence.

1929–1932

The German government continues to flounder. Meanwhile, the Nazis rise to become the most numerous party in the Reichstag.

1932

Hitler runs for president. Though he loses, the election cements the Party's importance in German politics.

1932 The Nazis do well enough in parliamentary elections to dominate the Reichstag.

1933 Hitler becomes chancellor of Germany. His powers steadily grow until he becomes a dictator.

1935 Nuremberg Laws passed, legalizing discrimination against Jews.

1938 *Kristallnacht,* or the Night of Broken Glass. Jews all across Germany are beaten, robbed, and killed. Germans troops enter Austria, taking over the country. In October, they occupy the Sudetenland in Czechoslovakia.

1939 Germany invades Poland on Sept. 1. Poland falls before the end of the month.

1940 Germany invades France, Belgium, Holland, and Luxembourg. All fall quickly.

1941 Hitler invades the Soviet Union. Special units follow the troops into Russia and begin killing communist leaders and Jews. It may have been in December of this year that Hitler decided to exterminate all of Germany's Jews.

1942   Mass exterminations at death camps
in German-held territory begin.

1943   The tide of the war has turned with
the German defeat at Stalingrad. The
Final Solution continues.

1944   Russia threatens Germany's borders.
The American and British armies land
in France. The Holocaust continues.

1945   The Allies close in on Germany. With
Russian troops only a few blocks
away, Hitler commits suicide
in Berlin.

Glossary

anti-Semitism
Hatred of Jews. One of the prime causes of the rise of the Nazis and the Holocaust.

Aryans
Term used by Hitler and others to describe the white "race" that included Germans. The term has no biological foundation. Technically, it refers to people who spoke, or whose ancestors spoke, Indo-European languages.

concentration camps
General term for special prison compounds used by Nazis and overseen by the SS.

death camp
Concentration camps devoted to the immediate mass murder of Jews and others. Also known as extermination camps.

Einsatzgruppen
Special units that organized mass killings of Jews and others in occupied territories.

Final Solution
The term adopted by the Nazi government for the plan to kill all Jews in Europe.

Führer
The leader—that is, Adolf Hitler.

Gestapo
Feared secret police unit of the SS with broad powers. The name comes from *Geheime Staatspolizei,* or state secret police.

ghetto
An area of a city set aside for a certain group of people. During World War II, the Germans established ghettos in occupied countries to help prepare for the elimination of Jews.

Holocaust
Term adopted by historians to describe the mass extermination and murder of Jews by Nazis.

Mein Kampf
Hitler's famous book laying out his "philosophy." Written while he was in jail for trying to overthrow the government.

Nazis
General term for Germans and others who
followed Hitler. Specifically, Nazis were
members of the National Socialist German
Workers' Party, NASDAP, which Hitler led.

putsch
An armed takeover of the government. Hitler
attempted a putsch in Munich in 1923. It
became known as the Beer Hall Putsch because
the government leaders were arrested in a large
beer hall.

Reichstag
The German parliament.

SA
The *Sturmabteilung*, or "storm detachment." Also
known as the "Brownshirts." Nazi Party
organization headed by Ernst Röhm for much
of the 1920s and early 1930s until the Night of
the Long Knives, when Röhm was arrested and
killed. The SA were often used to intimidate
enemies and fight with the police and
communists. Brownshirts also attacked Jews.

SS
The *Schutzstaffel*, or guard unit of the Nazi
Party. Members swore personal allegiance to
Adolf Hitler.

For More Information

Organizations

Holocaust Education Foundation
P.O. Box 6153
Newport News, VA 23606-6153
e-mail: info@holocaust–trc.org
Web site: http://www.holocaust–trc.org

United States Holocaust Memorial Museum
100 Raoul Wallenberg Place SW
Washington, DC 20024-2126
Web site: http://www.ushmm.org

Web Sites

Cybrary of the Holocaust
http://www.remember.org

Fortunoff Video Archive for Holocaust Testimonials
Yale University Library
http://www.library.yale.edu/testimonies

History Place: World War II in Europe
http://www.historyplace.com/worldwar2/

The Holocaust Chronicle
http://www.holocaustchronicle.org

The Holocaust History Project
http://www.holocaust-history.org

Holocaust Pictures Exhibition
http://www.fmv.ulg.ac.be/schmitz/holocaust.html

The Holocaust/Shoah Page
http://www.mtsu.edu/~baustin/holo.html

The Nizkor Project
http://www.nizkor.org

Simon Wiesenthal Center
Museum of Tolerance Online
http://motlc.wiesenthal.org

Stephen Spielberg Jewish Film Archive
http://sites.huji.ac.il/jfa

A Teacher's Guide to the Holocaust
http://fcit.coedu.usf.edu/holocaust

The Trial of Adolf Eichmann.
A companion Web site to the two-hour PBS
documentary.
http://www.pbs.org/eichmann

The Trial of German Major War Criminals
Includes the judgment of the International Tribunal.
http://www.nizkor.org/hweb/imt/tgmwc

Yad Vashem
Holocaust Martyrs and Heroes
     Remembrance Authority
http://www.yad-vashem.org

For Further Reading

Byers, Ann. *The Holocaust Overview*. Springfield, NJ: Enslow Publishers, 1998.

Dupuy, Trevor Nevitt. *The Military Life of Adolf Hitler, Führer of Germany*. New York: Franklin Watts, 1969.

Frank, Anne. *Diary of a Young Girl: The Definitive Edition*. New York: Doubleday, 1995.

Heyes, Eileen. *Adolf Hitler*. Brookfield, CT: The Millbrook Press, 1994.

Matas, Carol. *Daniel's Story*. New York: Scholastic, 1993.

Meltzer, Milton. *Never to Forget: The Jews of the Holocaust*. New York: Harper and Row, 1976.

Owens, Jesse, with Paul Neimark. *Jesse: The Man Who Outran Hitler*. New York: Fawcett Gold Medal, 1978.

Serotta, Edward. *Out of the Shadows*. New York: Birch Lane Press, 1991.

———— *Germans and Jews: A Photographic Diary*. Berlin: Nicolaische Verlagsbuchhandlung, 1996.

Sierakowiak, Dawid. *The Diary of Dawid Sierakowiak: Five Notebooks from the Lodz Ghetto*. New York: Oxford University Press, 1996.

Spiegelman, Art. *Maus*. New York: Pantheon
    Books, 1986.
Wiesel, Elie. Night. New York: Bantam Books, 1982.

For Advanced Readers

Bauer, Yehuda. *A History of the Holocaust*. New
    York: Franklin Watts, 1982.
Fest, Joachim C. *Hitler*. New York: Vintage
    Books, 1975.
Heiber, Helmut. *Adolf Hitler: A Short Biography*.
    London: Oswald Wolff Limited, 1972.
Schlant, Ernestine. *The Language of Silence: West
    German Literature and the Holocaust*. New York:
    Routledge, 1999.
Sibyll, Claus, and Jochen von Lang, ed. *Eichmann
    Interrogated: Transcripts from the Archives of the
    Israeli Police*. New York: Da Capo Press, 1999.

Film and Video

The Holocaust—In Memory of Millions, 1993.
    Narrated by Walter Cronkite. Documentary
    overview of Holocaust.
Night and Fog, 1955. Classic documentary by
    director Alain Resnais, still rated among best
    films on Holocaust. Subtitled.

Index

About the Author

Jeremy Roberts has written several biographies for young people, including works on Joan of Arc and Oskar Schindler.

Photo Credits

Cover image and p. 9 © Corbis; p. 13 © United States Holocaust Memorial Museum (USHMM); p. 14 © Staatsarchiv Bamberg, courtesy of USHMM Photo Archives; p. 25 © Yad Vashem Photo Archives, courtesy of USHMM; pp. 33, 37, 89, 91 © Archive Photos; p. 39 © Hulton-Deutsch Collection/Corbis; p. 41 ©Christel Gerstenberg/Corbis p. 51 © B.I. Sanders, courtesy of USHMM; p. 56 © National Museum of American Jewish History, courtesy of USHMM; pp. 62 and 64 © National Archives; p. 69 © National Archives, courtesy of USHMM; p. 71 © Richard A. Ruppert, courtesy of USHMM; pp. 79, 81 © Instytut Pamieci Narodowej/Institute of National Memory, courtesy of USHMM; p. 82 © George Kadish, courtesy of USHMM; p. 95 © Popperfoto/Archive Photos.

Series Design

Cynthia Williamson